Celestial Euphony

Poems by

Martin Elster

Plum White
Press

Published by Plum White Press LLC

For information concerning reprints, email: admin@poetrynook.com

ISBN-13:   978-1-939832-16-0
ISBN-10:   1-939832-16-0
LCCN: 2019919472
BISAC: Poetry / General

Cover painting "Mekheski – Moon People" by Nicholas Roerich, 1915. Cover design by Frank Watson.

Published in the United States of America.

For more on Plum White Press, please visit:

www.PoetryNook.com

A collection of over 300,000 classic poems in English, Chinese, Japanese, and other languages.

Free poetry contests with weekly and annual prizes.

for Elisa

Her garden's crammed with plants galore,
    each vying for her notice
as in a state of silent war,
    longing to be the lotus.

With the world her garden, she's swell as a swan
    on a lake in south Australia.
Though she likes to fly and is often gone,
    as a friend, she'll never fail ya!

Table of Contents

Celestial Euphony

Celestial Euphony

As dark and distant spheres resound like whale song in our ears
    and cosmic microwaves caress our spirit,
we pioneer, alone, across infinities of tone,
    amazed that we're the only ones who hear it.

While we glide amid the planets plump as plums and pomegranates,
    sailing with the interstellar current,
the sounds we make are quiet or they're louder than a riot,
    but for grooving, neither's ever a deterrent.

With clari-snare and flute-o-phone and tromba-sax and lute,
    xylo-horn and cymbal-harp and cello,
we shake our little craft with a great hurricane-like draft,
    cacophonous while synchronously mellow.

There's no one at the wheel; the skipper capers to a reel,
    a jig, flamenco, jota, or a salsa.
While galaxies collide, we're absolutely occupied
    as we zip through space in a ship as light as balsa.

If we chance on a black hole and, inattentive, lose control,
    free-falling ever faster in its eddy,
we won't freak out or panic, we will go on being manic
    till the cosmos bellows, "Guys, enough already!"

A Jump-Off Place

The people in the Middle Ages knew
the earth is round, but what they didn't know
is that the cosmos swells like sourdough
and that a time would come when men peer through
thirteen billion years to see the glow
of fuzzy islands near the very brink
of all creation. Who would ever think
we'd hear its echo on the radio?

Yet, though we've savored soupçons of that drink
distilled from centuries of observation,
the sudden knowledge of acceleration
has hurled us back to blackness in a blink.
Dark energy, comprising most of space,
means all we've learned is but a jump-off place.

A link

Evolution implies there's a link
between us and the germs in our sink;
   but my friend, rest her soul,
   had not washed her soup bowl,
and her "kin" bumped her off in a wink.

A New Lease

You offered me a brand new lease
along with a large rent increase,
but since I am no Rockefeller,
I'll soon be moving from your cellar.

I will not miss the lack of heat
in winter when my hands and feet
are fish and frogs beneath ice water
cold enough to kill an otter.

I will not miss the airlessness
inside this cave in summer, less
the motorcycles, sirens, horns
far more injurious than thorns.

Nor will I long to hear the noise
of babies, toys, and rowdy boys
that make the ceiling's floorboards rattle
as if from hooves of panicked cattle.

This pad's become a jumbo drum,
their frightful pan-de-mo-ni-um
more wounding of my calm than curses
(through which I've, somehow, written verses).

One matter, though, will cause me worry:
my tiny pals that perch or scurry.
House spiders, cellar spiders, small
as atoms, big as moons, they crawl

4

or dangle, hunt like wolves at night,
rappel down walls, or just sit tight.
I'm troubled when, for weeks, no patter
of bug feet nears a starved one's platter.

I know that you'll exterminate
my roommates when you renovate.
No, I won't go! I'll pay the rent
and deem those greenbacks quite well-spent!

A Preschooler Dwelleth Above

I fell asleep at 3:00 a.m.
and when I was in deepest REM
a boulder from a cloud of lead
hit the floor above my bed.

Every hair rose on my hide
as though a yeti got inside,
the panic-stricken face of night
fled and left the room too light,

and dreams I had of steamy trysts
faded like the morning mists.
Was it a boot, a building block
or Punch & Drop that made that knock?

Although he wakes me up each day
with toys like titans rough at play,
I always get to bed too late
and, consequently, don't get eight.

I'm fortunate if I get four.
I will get back at him. It's war!
I'll make him hear what he inspired.
(Well, maybe not. I'm way too tired.)

A Summer Songster

Just up ahead, beneath the streetlights' glare,
a splendid, fragile thing who's left his bed
of earth now stands with wide-set eyes to stare
up from the pavement, eyes that should have led
him to a trunk. Still, out of his broad head,
they scrutinize the steamy atmosphere
for somewhere he may vibrate, buzz, and wed
his song to summer, soon to disappear.

His veiny wings, transparent as the air,
great glassy shields, have hardened since he shed
his stiff, confining jacket to declare
he has arrived where any tramp could tread
and, with one careless footstep, leave him dead
as his discarded skin. But since I'm near,
I'll help him with his pilgrimage instead.
He'll sing of summer, soon to disappear.

It's me and him—whose visits are as rare
as gnats on Neptune. Pansy blossoms—red,
white, yellow, orange, violet—everywhere
adorn the yards and lanes, so many spread
with toxicants by those who have a dread
of patchy grass, beneath which, year by year,
strange beings grow, then clamber free, sap-fed,
to sing a tune that soon will disappear.

Black prince, you study me, but could have fled.
You drone. Crawl up onto my palm. No fear.
We reach an oak, where you'll pick up the thread.
Your kind will croon—while we all disappear.

7

A Tufted Titmouse Braves a Cold Spell

Peter-peter-peter cries my voice
echoing through the trees. Flakes fall to test
my stamina and patience. It is cold.
Tomorrow will be chillier still, fresh rime
glazing flower and fence. My whistles chime
like piccolos to pierce the stale and old
that clings as lichen to a larch. I rest
in a nest in a lifeless oak. I have no choice
but to sing and to hole up in this secondhand
woodpecker's dimple, no alternative
but to twitter to my better half, to live
in my feathered fashion. Oh, but it is grand
and it is hard and it's both work and play
and—*peter-peter*—it is cold today.

After Studying the Hubble Ultra-Deep Field

(Rondeau Redoublé)

"Once upon a time, faint lumps of light—
coiled bluish millipede, plump tawny snail—
each formed of scores of flames, whose rays took flight
soon after the Bang, appeared exquisite and frail

as spores," you muse as you tramp along this trail
through oak and hickory filtering the might
of the low-slung sun. You're lost in a fairy tale
of once-upon-a-time, as flecks of light

wink softly from radio towers on the height
like fireflies sparking the dusk. A fingernail
of moon appears while, beyond a long-winged kite,
coiled bluish millipede, plump tawny snail—

invisible as viruses—glide and sail
on waves of ion seas. How did the night,
beyond a jet plane's woolly water tail,
form multitudes of flames whose rays took flight?

You suddenly catch sight of a wary white-
tailed doe and her fawns, which follow without fail
as without fail the world became just right,
just right for a bang, a bang zapping the frail

and exquisite, as exquisite as the pale
but darkening skyline. Somewhere out of sight
a hoot owl harmonizes with the wail
of air-raid sirens. Things were looking bright
once upon a time.

After the Snowstorm

Is it a Chevy or a bear
beneath that hulking heap of snow,
hibernating in its lair?

If it's alive, its breaths are slow
as ice floes on Europa's seas.
It shall keep dozing; I'll not go

and dig it out today when trees
all tremble in their talcum dress.
Light paws and hiking boots now breeze

around the neighborhood. O bless
the snowplows! Sidewalks everywhere
are unobstructed (more or less).

I muse while breathing bracing air:
why bug a sleeping Chevy-bear?

Albert Einstein (1879-1955)

A young-looking fellow employed
as a patent assessor enjoyed
   experiments done
   in his head—lots of fun
for a purposeful, smart anthropoid.

He rode a light beam, thought of clocks
and a man in a plummeting box,
   but had very cold toes—
   which is just how it goes
when forgetting to bring your wool socks.

Views of gravity, light, time and space
were suddenly new, and his face
   became famed as a lion
   and the stars of Orion
which, unlike his hair, know their place.

Ambling

Wandering as my forebears did, without
religion, politics, agendas, hate,
ambling across this meadow, roaming about
these groves, around that lake, I gravitate
toward nothing particular—just time for smelling
the bogs and butterfly bushes; to touch those rushes,
their texture smooth as frogs; to probe this dwelling
of excellent insects; to listen to the thrushes
that pierce this fog, this cloud of quietude
guarding and sheltering these hills and fields.
I say, let there be quakes and hurricanes.
Let oceans rise. Let folks be kind or rude.
Those things are but the vague and far-off peals
of thunder and the cries of distant trains.

An Early Autumn Chill

Though bit by bit the mullein blossoms wither
and daisy fleabane slowly turns to seed,
white cabbage butterflies still sip the liquor
of clover—skipping, capering, keen to breed.

While sunflowers hang their heads to catch the murmur
of bumblebees, and pumpkins put on weight,
woolly bears, fueled up on summer's flora,
seek a secret place to hibernate.

Vast hordes of them are crushed on roads and highways,
quite out of harmony with human haste,
their bristles useless, too, against the sparrows
which love them (though it's an acquired taste).

Should they cocoon, they will emerge next April
and roam the night when bats are on the prowl,
yet few will fill the bellies of those mammals
which do not savor the flavor of bugs so foul.

Fields team with asters mimicking the sun god
with myriad rays of brilliant blue or pink
and eyes of gold to charm the pollinators
as day by day the region's rations shrink.

Gone are the cardinal's whistle, the hummer's hustle,
the robin's comical hops across the lawn,
the mockingbird's adroit impersonations.
So deafening, this quietude at dawn!

Black-eyed Susans drop their lemon petals,
Sol is sinking fast behind the hill,
milkweed down is hovering and dancing,
and chickadees fluff their feathers against the chill.

An Understanding

A dog flies at the flock, which mounts the air
like a huge, blaring, squawking herbivore
in search of forage. A great thunder-roar
emerges from below. Amid the glare
of winter sun as red as a ruby eye,
they catch sight of what seems to be a hawk
in silhouette. It rushes at the flock
tornado-like and wipes them from the sky.

Out of that sky the Airbus starts to drop,
its matching maws now choked and gorged with feather
and flesh. Sadly, there is no magic tether
from hawk to heaven to make its swan dive stop.
A cymbal clash proclaims a brutal landing
as man and bird come to an understanding.

Angel Wings

I come to Elizabeth Park to see him feed
from a bent lady's palm—a Canada goose
whose outward-angled wings (from too much bread),
like deadwood twigs, are of no earthly use.

He'd watched his flock take to the sky, and heard
their honks grow fainter, fainter . . . this wild bird
now nibbling oats and corn from a trembling hand
which got him through last winter on the pond.

Their common bond is clear as cloudless days,
solid as the crystal-covered oaks:
this longing for lost friends. No one will praise
her nurturing. Some night, a coon or fox
may catch him, or the elements may get him.
Yet watch him sidestep when she tries to pet him.

Anomaly

A girl has found a little frog
squatting on a rotting log,
its dewy body dozing there
as motionless as frozen air.

Impossible in this dim light
to learn it's an hermaphrodite,
incapable of procreation
due to freakish deviation

as it grew from tadpole stage
into a frog of legal age.
She goes to grab the beast. A hop.
The water puckers with a "plop!"

It got away from a child's clutch,
but not from mankind's toxic touch.

Cherry Blossom Reverie

On Hearing Keiko Abe Play the Marimba

As mallets frolic, leap and fall
and blur into a cloud of flowers,
the rosewood fills the spacious hall

with dazzling white sakura showers
borne from the tree we picnicked under,
all our minutes, all our hours

passing like this tuneful wonder
quickening my memory
and, wild as taiko-drumming-thunder,

we danced beneath that floral tree
that shook the garlands from its hair.
That night I dreamed a glorious sea

of petals washed ashore, the air,
the land, our very souls in thrall
to blossoms blowing everywhere.

I see you whirling in the squall
as mallets frolic, leap and fall.

Connecticut

We folks in Connecticut adhere to good etiquette,
  never covet, philander, or kill.
No one ever comes late to their job in this state
  and we never miss work 'cause we're ill.

Our vista's are stunning, and no one's seen running
  from robber or rapist or bum.
Everyone smiles. None lack domiciles.
  You won't see a soul looking glum.

Neither slum nor a mansion nor urban expansion
  you'll find in this fabulous region.
No one's ever pugnacious; instead, we're all gracious,
  with affordable health food stores legion.

Our cars don't pollute, all the women are cute,
  and the men are all free of addiction.
All our children are smart as Curie or Descartes,
  and I am the King of Pure Fiction.

Dino Air

Two hundred million years ago
the world was damp as dew and hot
and pterosaurs were soaring. No
expert can say precisely what
caused creatures to grow so darned colossal.
(Hard to tell from a tight-lipped fossil.)

Far lower in oxygen, that air
was good enough for dinosaurs.
Red tongues of lava licked the bare
and verdant spots alike. The jaws
of giant chasms opened wide
and life was in for a bumpy ride.

After Pangaea's porcelain crust
cracked up, each crenulated coast
was overcome with wanderlust.
Ammonites, in the nethermost
sea basins, loved their briny tub
and the globe was a jet-set dino club.

It happened like a lightning strike—
an earthward-tumbling boulder struck
the world, which bonged like a gong and shook,
and the ruling brutes ran out of luck,

save one warm-blooded breed we've met
that winged its way to us: the bird.

Feral and free or a caged pet,
observed in rainbow hues or heard,
it's a modern dinosaur. They dwell
on land, in oceans, breathing well

the breezes rich in oxygen.
They plunge off floes into frigid seas,
trill all night (to my wife's chagrin),
hover and hum like bumblebees,
gallop like colts across dry plains,
or bash their brains on windowpanes.

The world was hot and damp as dew.
Though cooler now, it's warming fast
as the swiftest falcon through the blue.
How long will this clement coolness last?
Will Earth, our avian pals, and we
return to dino air? We'll see.

Earth For Sale

We've just received our largest shipment ever of blue skies.
   Come check them out before you leave the system!
But if, instead of atmosphere, you crave a nice sunrise,
   we've got so many styles. In fact, I'll list 'em:

The types from airborne particles or molecules of air,
   volcanic ash trapped in the troposphere
and cloud and Rayleigh scattering. We guarantee you'll stare.
   That isn't what you want? Then do not fear.

This planet sports so many things of interest and worth:
   countless kinds of animals and plants
and rocks containing jewels. You never know what you'll unearth.
   You'll long to live here after just one glance.

Too many folks, you say? You think this planet isn't well?
   Just look around. Behold the majesty.
From Everest to Death Valley, this world has no parallel.
   Oh, please don't go! We'll give it to you free!

Falling More Slowly

I fall and fall yet never touch the ground,
where the unfinished story of our race
(together with all living creatures bound
to a revolving oblate rock) takes place.
I go on falling round and round and round
that breathing boulder at the perfect pace
as not to tumble toward it or to rush
away to Mars or to the stars. A hush

pervades the universe beyond my air
while winds of ghostly plasma hurry on.
Thinner than the peel of a russet pear,
the rim of Earth's a band of blue at dawn
which, bit by bit, erases every flare
of sleeping cities. I'm a soaring swan,
far from all woes, filled with sanguinity,
one with the distant flames of infinity.

Giordano Bruno (1548-1600)

Folks reckoned the Earth is so rare
that the rest of all space must be bare
    and empty of creatures,
    but among all their teachers
one asserted what most wouldn't dare.

That philosopher's surname was Bruno.
His claim? We're not numero uno
    and each star is a sun—
    that there's not merely one
but bajillions!—a thing we now *do* know?

But for a heretical scholar,
it could be quite risky to holler
    that we're not the hub
    of existence, 'cause, bub,
you will blaze from your shoes past your collar.

He Goes on Glowing

The Sun was low with a blinding glow,
    the stoplight silhouetted.
You had to squint through the windshield's glint
    and slowed a bit and fretted,
since you couldn't discern in the Sun's bright burn
    if the light was green or red.
Though it couldn't be seen, you guessed it was green,
    which nearly made you dead.

For you sped straight through—your car just flew!—
    and crashed and bashed and banged
into another. The jolt. Oh, brother!
    The metal—how it clanged!
Though the cars were stilled, no one was killed,
    just shaken up like a gong
pelted by hail, or reeds in a gale.
    Yet who was in the wrong?

A copper came, thought, "Who to blame?"
    made many an observation;
said, "It's no use, I can't deduce
    the cause and write a citation."
Then you gazed at the sky with a squinty eye
    and knew on whom to place
the blame. Oh, yes, he'd never confess,
    yet flaunts his fulgent face.

It was the Sun—that son of a gun—
    that gaseous, jumbo ball
who warms the Earth and gives life birth,
    yet doesn't care at all
'bout folks in cars or flies in jars
    or kids with sunlit kites.
He goes on glowing while ferns are growing
    and fools run traffic lights.

Helen Keller (1880-1968)

Your eyesight and hearing were gone,
yet you felt just as blithe as a fawn
   when you learned that a word
   could stand for a bird
or the flowers that bloomed in your lawn.

The very first word that you learned
was "water." Thereafter you yearned
   for more, and then more
   till the letters would pour
from your soul into books, finely turned.

Face the sunshine and you will not see
the shadow, you said, for the key
   to happiness lies
   in kindness. Not eyes
nor ears, but your dreams made you free.

July Musings

A hundred thousand million galaxies
in motley clusters rapidly receding
from one another—like a bunch of bees
repelled by tainted nectar they'd been eating—
is a sure sign the cosmos is inflating,
as is the vocal structure of the frog
now calling out across the water, waiting,
as patient as the shadows in this bog.
With every croak, his throat must grow then shrink.
But will that happen to the universe?
Well, you can speculate and muse and think
and theorize and wonder and immerse
your thoughts in such abstract considerations
while I sit listening to frog vibrations.

Long-Distance Relationship

The planet takes nine hundred thousand years
to orbit the small orb that is her light.
Though practically free-floating, a loose bond
connects the couple. No refulgent spheres
ever visit. Never-ending night
engulfs that world of winter, far beyond
the mass of Jupiter—a giant's giant.
In their long-distance dalliance, world and star
circumgyrate, aching to embrace.
Their tie is tenuous, a link reliant
on faith a sun won't pass too near and jar
the planet into interstellar space.
Yet in the face of time's eternal frost
they vow their love will never be star-crossed.

Lovebugs (Plecia nearctica)

A flurry grays the April air
as clouds of speckles swirl and mate,
euphoric, blazing, unaware

of windshields on the interstate
hurtling through their fevered storm.
These whirlwind-wings pursuing their fate,

in red and black above the warm
blacktop, link and live three days.
Tripping on truck exhaust, they swarm,

convinced it's flora which decays.
They catch the fumes, sweet as the spice
of rot, home in on motorways

and, as they're turned to mush, think, "Nice!—
manure, grass clippings—paradise!"

Meditation on a Twilight Union

Luminous, numinous,
Venus and Jupiter
triangle-set with a
    scimitar moon:
soon they'll descend into
invisibility;
stars will appear and the
    crickets will croon.

Vega, Arcturus, and
countless bright crystals will
quiver the heavens and
    dazzle the eye.
Journey your eyes to the
phantasmagorical
reaches of space and your
    spirit might fly!

Alpha Centauri, Ca-
nopus, Capella: stars
incontrovertibly
    gave us all birth;
Ponder the chill of deep
space, though, your mind will then
unhesitatingly
    kiss Mother Earth!

Mermaids Are Waiting for You!

It sat there on the strand that day,
  a day that viewed strange meetings.
He picked it up from where it lay
on grit and pebbles, wet from spray,
  bruised by the breakers' beatings.

He held it up against an ear,
  an ear drenched by the thunder
of muted oceans, far and near—
a pink-lipped conch, a souvenir
  he thought, until from under

its briny, salmon-colored sound,
  a sound unlike the ocean:
a voice that told him it was bound
to whale and seal, and never drowned,
  except in strong emotion.

"Let's meet beyond the reef," it purred,
  those purring tones erotic
as Amphitrite's, every word
exotic as a coral-bird,
  each sea-lynx growl hypnotic.

The bathers, boats, the heavens' eye
  (an eye half-closed and Titian),
rendering the western sky
so roseate, its hues would vie
  with a Turner exhibition,

to him were distant as the flight,
  the flight of a shearwater.
"I am a mermaid of the night,
whose tail is fashioned to excite.
  I frisk with eel and otter."

Waves drummed, but he just heard that arch,
  that arch, coquettish timbre.
He thought he heard the wedding march
by Mendelssohn. No hint of starch
  in that coy voice. "I'm Amber."

While plovers piped and seagulls squawked—
  squawked like the world's noisemakers—
and other seabirds plunged or flocked,
he chucked that ornate shell and walked
  straight into the breakers.

Out past the reef he met his fate,
  a fate with flowing tresses.
The sea-beast didn't hesitate
to wrap her tail around her date
  and drown him in caresses.

Microchiroptera

No microchiropteran ever complains
when the rawness of autumn creeps into the day,
his arthropod prey having fluttered away.
With his pals he piles into a cave, then abstains
from all food while he hangs like a fuzzball. The pains
he's taken to gain a few grams in the May
of his bug-catching bustle will, hopefully, play
in his favor, reviving him after the rains
and the blizzards retreat. Then, with luck, when the leaves
begin to uncurl in the bright vernal suns,
diaphanous pinions unfurl, and the sheaves
of packed bodies disperse into twilight's cool breath.
Moths and beetles, look out! For exuberance runs
intense in his blood as he seeks for your death.

My Dream of Being a Leaf-cutter Ant

I dream of building a subsurface maze,
scooping out loads of earth, constructing roads,
great humps and hills and highways. Holidays
are absent from my dream. The warm abodes

I'll fashion from the soil will last for ages.
Born from an extraordinary mother,
my million kin and I will earn no wages
yet jolly in our job with one another.

We'll cut up leaves and lug them to our lair
and feed the greenery to wholesome fungi
gorged on by our larvae. We'll take care
of all our waste so nothing's ever grungy.

I dream I am an ant. I dream of leaves.
I dream I sip their sap and lap their juices.
I dream that each of us (big, small) receives
just treatment from the queen, which reproduces

enough to keep alive the colony—
a colony which trumps the human race.
Olympian limbs rocket me up a tree
and all my sisters' faces are *my* face.

Neil Armstrong (1930-2012)

You could fly while still growing and green,
could repair any flying machine
   by your twenties, and tested
   new rocket planes, crested
the clouds in your bright X-15.

In due course, you were picked for Apollo
(undreamed of by falcon or swallow)
   to land on the moon,
   and to do it quite soon
so the Commies could no more than follow.

You touched the moon's hide, took a stride,
spoke of steps and of leaps, then all pride
   disappeared as you turned
   toward your planet and learned
that your thumb is precisely as wide!

No Whiners

Gratitude is a leaf that laughs
   and falls up toward the sun
and glides and soars like a red-tailed hawk
   whose heart won't be undone

by clouds as inky as the jaws
   of a giant carnivore.
It never wants to land on earth,
   in oak or sycamore,

but keeps ascending, drifting, wheeling
   over the hills and fields
and thinks a cyclone sounds as fine
   as a thousand glockenspiels.

It laughs with the glee of a major key,
   though the world's so full of minor,
and goes on hovering and gliding
   beyond the last airliner.

Gratitude is not a whiner.
   Gratitude will not moan.
While awestruck by the universe,
   how can it feel alone?

Noise Pollution

Nayana walks along the byway,
Overhearing the chatter of
Impassioned passerines, while highway
Sounds upstage and rudely shove
Entrancing trills aside. Bird-twitter
Pokes and punches through noise-litter
Of rig, shrill siren, motorbike.
Let every sparrow have a mic!
Let every robin sing and chirrup
Unabashedly, each bright
Timbre be a blade and bite
Into the blare so it will clear up.
Observing the clash of chirp and din,
Nayana hopes the birds will win.

Odd?

I fear snakebites,
dogs with no hair,
meteorites,

shrill siren-blare,
and my neighbor, Todd.
Why do you care?

You think I'm odd,
a piece of work,
but like my bod.

There are some jerks
who throw a fit
and go berserk

and start to hit
for the slightest thing.
Akin to a pit

viper's sting,
the venomous words
they often fling

are no more absurd
than your attack
of this brittle bird.

Your frightful flak's
like a feline's hiss.
I rub your back,

yet you won't kiss
me anymore.
Oh, what is this,

this stuff you pour
like acid rain
upon the shore

of my migraine?
Oh, why do you go
to your cousin, Jane's,

with me as though
I were still your mate?
I just don't know

why you'd want a date
with such a freak
with all those traits

you hate. My beak's
too big. Big deal!
So for a week

I've worn high heels.
For three whole nights
I've had no meals.

I fear bright lights
and lofty heights,
but my biggest fright?
Your slightest slight!

Ode to the Tardigrade

Tardigrade on the Moon—
will you perish soon?
Parked in her immense
left eye, you have the sense

(since there is neither air
nor moss nor water there)
to curl into a ball,
dry out and, thus, forestall

the death that would ensue
for anyone but you.
A wizard at survival
you've not a single rival,

for when an asteroid
dives headlong from the void
and pummels us, you'll chuckle
as we collapse and buckle.

For half a billion years
through sea-changed biospheres,
you've been here. There's no doubt
your mastery stands out,

your expertise at cheating
the Reaper as you're heating
to feverish degrees
or cooling down to freeze

(without so much as sneezing,
shivering, or wheezing)
to paralyzing zero.
And so, my tiny hero,

when we again alight
upon the Moon some night,
be kind and do not chortle
at souls so frail and mortal!

Pyrotechnics

The heavens effervesced with smoke and noise
as spiders, peonies, and palms enthralled
the mobs of men and women, girls and boys,

but shocked the foxes, rabbits, deer, and mauled
the air like ack-ack fire. It spooked the bats
while coons abandoned kits and field mice crawled

down burrows. Even butterflies and gnats
behaved as if huge bolides overhead
were quaking space-time. Humans have their spats,

but this seemed more like war. Some birds dropped dead,
some lost their hearing; dogs were hit by cars
or disappeared, while other creatures bled,

pulled through and lived, disfigured, etched with scars
to face anew this fête beneath the stars.

Reservoir No. 6

Geese dawdle near the melting ice
   while gulls, like white confetti,
wheel before a mount of mist:
   they sense the sun is ready
to muscle through the pall of clouds
   whose drops have drummed as steady

across these hills as ocean waves
   have clawed the cliffs, as streams
have swelled, and wind has gnawed the world.
   They've washed away the dreams
of tadpoles, catfish, carp, and trout
   which flash their glitter-gleams.

Defrosted frogs in fevered ferver
   quack and trill and whistle,
fawns tail their leaders through the cedars,
   blinking at bears that bristle,
while hairy caterpillars hatch
   on hickory and thistle.

This must be why I scaled the fence,
   slogging along a track
of rills and muddy puddles; why
   each sneaker is a sack
of sopping wilderness; and why
   each spring I will be back.

Rockledge: Winter Trails

A luster plays across the glaze
on crusts and bombes and parallel lines
from skis that glided past the pines
lolling in Earth's lantern-rays.

While a red-tailed hawk wheels round, wild geese,
with jet-black heads and white chinstraps
and squawks and honks and vigorous flaps,
mount a wind that won't release

the region from its spell, like vines
wrapped round the maples, oaks, and willows.
The rubescent sun, unobscured by billows,
reflecting off the trail that winds

around this tract of land, descends—
a precipitous and fiery dive.
You wonder if you will arrive
before this blustery evening ends,

when Venus starts to scintillate
and foxes leave their lairs to stalk
the voles; as hungry as the hawk,
they'll hunt as in the primal state.

Although the dark will soon devour
the way, you linger—and you dally
through the stillness of this valley,
draped in winter's fleeting hour.

Slack Traffic

This is the slackest traffic I have been in.
And yet I'm fairly confident I'm winning
the battle between ecstasy and languor,
the deathmatch between sanity and anger.
I drive so slowly, I could fall asleep
but, gazing at a Shangri-La of sheep
grazing tranquilly across the street
is good as savoring a frozen treat.
Though tentacles of heat from every car
try murdering my mood, the finches are
so free and high above this hellish jam,
I've almost lost the sense of where I am—
some planet parallel to this old sphere,
a world where horns don't blare, the air is clear,
where narrow tracks of asphalt don't confine us,
where fumes which spew from rigs don't plague my sinus.
So long have I been loitering in this mess,
I've missed my own recital. I can guess
my guzzler will keep guzzling for some time.
So I reach for a book. Is it a crime
to read while driving? Yes. But this ain't driving!
I haven't a notion when I'll be arriving
to where I'm headed. Reading is the thing
to do, or drum the dashboard while I sing
Rodolfo's aria from *La Bohème*.
At least I haven't drifted into REM,
though that may happen soon, for dusk has laid
its copper wings upon this slow parade,
which now has gone from turtle-speed to sloth,
my windshield host to a heedless hulking moth.

Snatched from the Farm: Three Sisters

1.

One line consists of elderly and ill;
the other young and fit and working age,
who'll get a bowl of drugged soup as their wage
and even get the hang of a new skill.
Two sisters in the "healthy" line now see
their sibling standing in the other row—
the sibling with the eczema. They know
that something doesn't look right here. The three
must walk or die together. They've no choice.
The youngest sprints across the yard to pull
the "sick" one back. The trains will soon be full,
and when they stop, nobody will rejoice.
They're off together rolling down the track,
three teens whose parents never will be back.

2.

As fodder for the factories, they trekked
barefoot across the snow fields. Hunks of bread
were all that kept their reed-like frames erect.
One bitter morning, just beneath their tread,
they noticed spuds and scooped them up. Those raw
tubers they'd conceal and eat at night,
aware their persecutors had a law
prohibiting these girls from such delight.
In camp that evening, lined up in the quad,
the sisters, close amid the others, shook
as one in ten were murdered by the squad.

When the girl beside them dropped, they didn't look,
but knew they had been spared. The following dawn
they held each other as they plodded on.

3.
They walked and slept, but didn't die together.
The Russians came and then the sisters set
their sights on Palestine, where each one met
a man, had kids, and then the crucial tether
that lasted through the horror snapped when two
stayed put and saw the youngest move away.
She watched her children blossom day by day
in a land of hope or, leastwise, somewhere new.
She and her family once owned a farm
in Bratislava. Now she's in a place
where caregivers abound. The human race
will kill or comfort, dish out food or harm.
She dreams now, not of trials and ordeals,
but of the cows, the chickens, and the fields.

So Much Depends

So much depends upon a German Shepherd,
a Vizsla, Collie, or this yellow Lab
beside the sightless lady who walks round
the streets and sidewalks of a megacity
as treacherous as black ice and as peppered
with poles and holes and bumps and curbs and cars
as space with comets, asteroids, and stars—
so different from those dog-less days as drab
as a book of empty pages and no plot.
With four good ears and six good feet they bound
along the lanes. Why pity them, this gritty
duo moving through this tangle fraught
with myriad risks? Do they appear to fear it?
How can they miss a step with such team spirit?

Sol Concealed

"How dare you block my blaze," Sun said to Moon,
"it's disrespectful." Moon ignored his whining,
continuing to move before his shining
indignant visage. The sunny afternoon
was swiftly growing moonless, and the stars
popped up across the sky with Saturn, Mars,

beige Jupiter, white Venus (a dazzling dot)
and even Mercury (infrequent guest)
along with the Great Canine in the west
(witnessed in the winter, not on hot
dog-day afternoons). Now Sun was seething
while we eyewitnesses were barely breathing.

The wind grew cold, birds took a power nap,
the crickets started quavering, and we
stood round, gaping and goggling in Tennessee,
pondering this otherworldly gap,
this discontinuation of the light.
Feeling effaced, Sun burned for a fiery fight.

What happened next was truly epoch-making.
Ceasing its mischief, by minute degrees
Moon slunk away. The world's hostilities
ended at once. No longer bellyaching,
Sun shone again in all its awesome glory,
forgetting that all things are transitory.

Somewhere Near You

They're hidden. They hear you. They lurk somewhere near you,
tingeing your thoughts with strange ink.
Mere shadows, they're crafty as crows and don't fear you
and if you found out there's no air on their sphere, you
would know those who lurk somewhere near you,
would goggle in wonder, or shrink.

They sail on the winds of the thirteenth dimension
like microbes adrift in your drink,
and slip through a chink with a single intention:
to snatch you by methods beyond comprehension.
And now in the thirteenth dimension
you're a conifer stalking a skink

while narwhals eat nectar and froghoppers ferret
for pebbles that thunder and plink,
where no one believes you however you swear it
and no one hears, "Help me!" however you blare it
(apart from the purple-winged ferret
who can hear every color but pink).

They glide through the shoals of your soul-mind or mosey
like numbats down runnels that slink
through the gloom of your room. At the moment you're cozy
in slumber or slouched on the couch getting dozy,
they glide or they zip or they mosey
and smirk while you sway on the brink.

Spring Peepers

Spring peepers trill and whistle in between
the avenue (where drivers rush toward shops),
construction site, the woods, the putting green.
No one stops to listen to these drops

of sentience small as buttercups and shrill
as piccolos. They hide amid the stalks
that rise up from a liquid eye as still
as a spyglass pointed at the equinox,

unblinking for eternity. The first
of April. The environs dance and ring
with notes from frogs who, though they're unrehearsed,
belt out a song precisely tuned to spring.

These lusty soon-to-be inamoratos,
iconic crooning harbingers, will soon
be silent. You who ride inside your autos,
roll down the windows! Do not wait till June!

Spring Will Leave You Behind

The thaw has drawn the robins, ravenous, eager
for things that creep, while terra firma teases
with wafts of geosmin, hints of the hocus-pocus
that brought the thundershower, woke the crocus,
and coaxed the chorus frogs to call, which breezes
convey like news. They've lived through winter's meager

provisions, trilling the nip out of their blood.
A cattail pond I walk by every day
already stirs with cyan, orange, gold
and reddish shapes. Your hypothermic hold
diminishes with each and every ray
that touches fur and feather, flower and bud.

I watch a balancing act above as chill
as were your rime-caked eyes: a soaring hawk,
its wings as motionless as your emotions,
scans the fields for mice. No magic potions
will bring you back. You've vanished in the talk
of the towhee and the whistling whip-poor-will.

Stridulation

The katydids all katydid,
    well-hid
on twigs of sycamores and birches,
    on perches
amid the leaves of oak and aspen,
    raspin'
like souls that briefly breathe, feet graspin'
the branches of these fleeting days
that will evaporate like haze,
    well-hid on perches, raspin'.

Each pulse that pierces through the dark,
    each spark
links this arboreal world to all.
    Each call,
when merged with all the other trills,
    rings hills.
Their predetermined insect wills,
like shooting stars, light up night's gloom
and touch the glow of Cygnus' plume.
    Each spark, each call rings hills.

That's Chemistry

Curious Curie, you played
　　with atoms as unstable
as a shaky surgeon, elements
　　as bad as Cain to Abel.

The isotopes you isolated
　　glowed like a warning label,
harming you even as they joined
　　the periodic table.

And yet, your inspiration's led
　　to novel therapies
and may fulfill your wish and bring
　　all cancers to their knees.

Ra-di-o-ac-tiv-i-ty—
　　the word cries, "Danger! Danger!"
But now the very sun itself
　　no longer is a stranger.

The Barking of the Dog

Why is the world so focused on the barking of the dog
    when the cosmos quakes with rattling station wagons,
huge mowers moaning, blowers droning, tools that cruelly dig,
    motorbikes that scream like raving dragons,

rigs rumbling over potholes, doors maniacally banging,
    jackhammers gouging roads that throb and rock,
jet aircraft booming, sirens yowling, railroad crossings clanging,
    the ice-cream trucks that drift down every block

repeating "Turkey in the Straw" or "Do Your Ears Hang Low"?
    While mobs engage in age-old sports like shouting,
while firecrackers burst and chainsaws roar and roosters crow,
    while gangs wage war upon the ghetto, shooting,

there comes a more abhorrent noise, a din without cessation,
    begun at dawn and going even now,
a strange and strident racket causing serious vexation—
    the voice of misery, going "bow-wow-wow."

The Black Dog of the Hanging Hills

The Black Dog of the Hanging Hills
   will tip its head to howl,
yet not a woof nor a whimper spills
   from him, not one faint growl.

He savors human company
   and charms you with sad eyes;
but when those orbs turn fiery,
   they herald your demise.

He leaves no prints in sand or snow,
   appears when the sun is bright,
or at dusk on a crest in the full moon's glow—
   ethereal as night.

It's said that long ago a pup
   that wandered with its master
en route to rugged heights trudged up
   a path, straight to disaster.

On the loftiest ledge its keeper lurched
   and plunged from ridge to gorge.
The mongrel, lost and restless, searched
   the woods for broken George,

but never found the man who'd reared
   and steered him through those wilds.
I'd hiked there once, and a dog appeared;
   it tagged along some miles,

beguiling me as it larked and leapt,
   then bounded off like a buck.
The next time it appeared, it crept
   in shadow. Terror-struck,

I lost my footing, nearly tumbled
   into a gulch; discerned
a phantom's gaze. My courage crumbled.
   Unruffled, I returned

one early April dawn to climb
   those treacherous traprock trails
where copperheads and deer kill time
   with toads and cottontails.

Hawks wheeled and whistled, corvids clamored,
   thrushes thrilled to fill
the ears of Earth, woodpeckers hammered—
   when all went suddenly still.

The cursed cur, his eyes cerise,
   materialized anew.
I free-fell, easy as the breeze.
   My backbone cracked in two.

My eyes flew open: there I saw
   the milky fangs of death,
watched venom dribbling from its maw,
   although I felt no breath.

Way up above us hung the cliff
   I fell from. Then I stirred
and rose, refreshed; I wondered if
   a time warp had occurred.

My steps, as light as a lunar cricket's,
   drew me toward the summit
far from the mass of tangled thickets.
   Flying! Soaring from it!

Now night and day and all year round
   I hike here with a breed
as black as ravens, hushed—a hound
   I never have to feed.

The Cymbal Player

As bows and fingers quiver strings,
as lungs and lips whip up the air,
as notes soar on great falcon wings,

one player, seated in his chair
like a finch hid in a maple tree,
as if the creature wouldn't dare

trill out above the symphony
(perhaps in fear of being caught
by a raptor high above the lea),

begins to rise like an afterthought
amid the pianissimos
and, like a hunter's rifle shot

as bright as ninety-nine rainbows
of overtones, he spreads, then hits
two plates together. The ether glows

like sunlight through the woods. He sits
back down. And yet the clang still rings
and darts and dances, flutters, flits

and, for the merest moment, clings,
then fades away like all brief things.

The Enigma of Time

Though there's barely a drop in the brooks and the creeks,
   nearly dry as the open-air pools,
time's protean arrow—today a bolero,
   tomorrow a jig—soon will cause
pears and apples to fall and leaf chaos to sprawl
   while the youth sit like jailbirds in schools.

Blue dragonflies dart above moss-covered ponds
   and on puddles the water bugs race
as speedily streaking for prey they are seeking
   near patches of soil and stones
as many an atom will, in an air stratum,
   whip round its cerulean space.

Though the days still feel warm as a dog's underbelly,
   night by night the crickets get colder,
their chirps getting slower, their pitch getting lower,
   till their silvery trills disappear
like the darners and birds rushing off with the words
   of the whispering trees—now bolder

than tanagers, soon to be balder than buzzards.
   While the daffodil eye in the sky
turns meeker and shyer—look!—higher and higher
   the stars of Orion will rise.
Then when wood frogs and peepers become frozen sleepers,
   they'll know they've no choice but to lie

under ice and to dream as they circle a star
   in a galaxy, whirling away
like a slow-spinning pail full of Newcastle ale
   or the sweep of the hands of a clock
or a sunflower's face as it swivels to chase
   that light every life must obey.

The Fledgling

Hopping around the parking lot,
oil-streaked and stovetop-hot,
her young ignores the shrieks of "danger
drawing near!" But I'm no stranger.

I've seen her perched atop the fence,
her deep red tint in evidence.
But when her fearless flyer smacks
a car, something in me reacts.

As she observes with anxious eye,
I clutch him close. He fights to fly
from fingers kind yet as unbending
as bone and not used to befriending

robins. But I rush to bring
this frightened one inside. I wing
it playing vet and stroke his head.
He shuts his eyes. He must be fed,

I know. She had been busy schooling
him to fly; now I sit fooling
with this vulnerable guest.
I'd set him free, but where's her nest?

How to lead him to grass and clover,
where fledglings will not be run over.
To guide him to the caterpillars.
To guard him from the robin killers.

The Great Wall of America

On a planet in a cosmos far away
there's a USA that's not the USA,
edged by a wall so ugly, Cooper's hawks
and vultures will not perch atop it. Flocks
of bats and buntings ram it, while the turtle
and turkey blink and boggle at that hurdle
whose stainless teeth impale the stratosphere,
whose reach makes creatures prisoners all year.
Poets and meditators often wake
with hearts and kidneys missing. A mistake?
or just a program glitch inside a dream
hammered into heads by the regime
which built that barrier? Not the fiercest gale
nor hurricane nor earthquake can upset it.
Even the butterflies, bees, and beetles dread it.
Jumbo jet or Zeppelin or kite—
none dare traverse it. With the appetite
of a thousand whales, it gulps them in a bite.
When master mountaineers attempt to scale
the wall, they fall, or languish in a jail
with all the rest who waste away inside
a country or a cooler and abide
by the common rules in a cosmos far away
where the USA is not the USA.

The Loneliest Road

Another planet grows and shrinks away,
the heliosphere an ebbing memory,
you streaking like a wayward gamma ray.
Around your vessel blooms a potpourri
of comet, nebula, dark energy
rushing you through the void, accelerating,
all you've ever cared for quickly fading.

What road is lonelier than the universe?
For decades one could sail and never stumble
across another soul. Things could be worse.
Distracted, you could accidentally bumble
too close to a cosmic gullet and wildly tumble,
yet really no more lost than where you coast
past eagle, spider, witch-head, horsehead, ghost.

Though wandering through space entails great risk,
you have no choice—the sun's begun to swell.
While moving at velocities as brisk
as jets of interstellar wind, you smell
the rabbitbrush, the desert breezes, dwell
on sounds of soughing yucca palms and creeks,
glimpse bighorn bounding boulders, rusty streaks

of sunsets. As you near the edge of space,
you think of the stone tools your forebears used
while breathing mayfly lives, a vanished race
in tune with wilderness; and, though you've cruised
for torrents of time now down this road suffused
with radiation, your single mutant eye
still sees, not stars, but fireflies in July.

The Mist

We danced that day as two who knew the mist.
As evening cooled the meadow drew the mist.

Orion shyly peeked above the ridge.
Cygnus, spread your wings, pursue the mist!

Each evening the red foxes roam the valley.
Like them, there was a time you knew the mist.

One night the moon came up, unrolled its rays.
A screeching raptor woke and slew the mist.

I called your name, called loud a thousand times!
A katydid responded through the mist.

Far-off, the owls tu-whit tu-whoo the mist.
They infiltrate my mind. I rue the mist.

The songbirds have all gone, the leaves have dried.
Only bats that dimly view the mist.

The breeze picked up across the distant hills.
None can remove the breath from you, the mist.

I watched a flock of martins heading south.
Then, clean away, a blizzard blew the mist.

The Pigeons

Close by the bridge, they javelin
the frosty blue. Flashing, fading,
dipping, climbing, as if to win
the Bird Olympics, emulating
their wild forebears, forever together,
bonded by the sturdy tether

of kinship. The townsfolk dare not bustle
about in gales. They're all shut in
like rabbits in their huts. The rustle
of remnant leaves and twigs is a thin
and bony xylophone. The flocking
aces wheel round and round the walking

man on the bridge, who watches each bird
click with the cloud in euphoric flight.
Strolling alone, for a moment cured
of the whiteness under the frigid light
of sunset, he can't help but stare
as spirits soar and fade and flare.

The Space Roadster

Elon, you've lost one of your cherry cars.
We doubt you miss it, though, for Starman steers it,
piercing the emptiness en route to Mars
and the ring of rocks beyond. What flyer fears it,

the absolute of space? Not *this* fake pilot!
Its gaze is black as the gaps between the stars,
and yet the worlds and suns seem to beguile it.
Who would have thought that dummies in red cars

could zip into earth orbit and keep going?
They flabbergasted us, your booster rockets
which settled like a pair of sparrows (owing
to bang-up engineering). In your pockets

were all the funds you needed for a test
that bested your most hopeful expectations.
Now car and mannequin are on a quest
to beat our wildest visualizations

as Earth recedes with all its blues and whites
as Mars grows closer with its browns and coppers
as space becomes spectacular with lights
as we audacious apes become star-hoppers.

The Timpanist

i.m. Alexander Lepak

No gauges graced those drums. No need to look
and check. He went on ear alone. The bowls
of hammered copper rumbled so they shook
the auditorium with thunder-rolls
or purred like surf-washed gravel, gently heaving.
We called him "Big Foot." Working the tuning pedals,
he managed, though a thousand themes were weaving
contrapuntal mischief round the kettles,
to nail his pitches. Lowering his nose
as if he were about to smell the skin
or whisper secrets to it—in this pose,
he'd flick it with a finger, tuning in
to harmony, polyphony and scale,
mount music's rolling cumuli, and sail.

The Woolly Bear

Along a silvan lane, you spy a critter
creeping with a mission, a woolly bear
fattened on autumn flora. So you crouch,
noting her triple stripes: the middle ginger,
each end as black as space. Her destination
is some unnoticed nook, a sanctuary
to settle in, greet the fangs of frost,
then freeze, wait winter out—lingering, lost
in dreams of summer, milkweed, huckleberry.
Though she's in danger of obliteration
by wheel or boot, your fingers now unhinge her.
She bends into a ball of steel. No "ouch"
from bristles on your palm as you prepare
to toss her lightly to the forest litter.

She flies in a parabola, and lands
in leaves. Though she has vanished, both your hands
hold myriad tiny hairs, a souvenir
scattered like petals. When this hemisphere
turns warm again, she'll waken, thaw, and feast
on shrubs and weeds (the bitterer the better)
then, by some wondrous conjuring, released
from larval life. At length she will appear
a moth with coral wings—they'll bravely bear
her through a night of bats or headlight glare,
be pulverized like paper in a shredder,
or briefly flare in a world that will forget her.

The World

Unlike the azure that protects the world,
the sky-dome's plexiglass reflects the world.

A spherical lab experiments for eons.
Slowly, the life it bears perfects the world.

Billions of bits of sparkle whirling, whirling.
Something's alive among these specks: the world.

A robed astronomer sees a curious glow
light up his globe as he dissects the world.

You shut the greenhouse windows one by one,
then wonder who it is that wrecks the world.

With a writ of attachment in its curved appendage,
the alien says it must annex the world.

Amphibians, mammals, reptiles, birds, fish, insects—
two by two a ship collects the world.

"Farewell," she said, and fled to a new planet.
He shrugs when queried, "Was your ex the world?"

Tumefied into a scarlet monster:
the sun. Nobody resurrects the world.

The astronaut, though warned she'll turn to salt,
glances back and recollects the world.

A cosmic magpie spies a blue-white marble,
then, comet-like, swoops down and pecks the world.

The Wright Brothers

Orville and Wilbur were right
that a flying machine could take flight.
   They spent money and years
    and, while they had fears,
they thought it might work. It just might!

To reach any meaningful height,
their engine, they knew, must be light.
   Then in 1903
    the seabirds would see
an odd and remarkable sight.

Though the ospreys and gulls saw them fly it,
most specialists didn't quite buy it:
   "How could wings, so unbendable,
    be somehow ascendable?"
Yet they were, and now none can deny it!

Upheaval

Buried in the Haiti earthquake of 2010, musician Romel
Joseph recalled concertos to keep his sanity.
—Miami Herald

Sibelius and Brahms will pull me through
the dark, the dust (though everywhere all strings
have snapped, gone mute)—and Beethoven—my true
companions. Once per hour my wristwatch rings

as if school were still in session. I remain
immobile, yet they're bound to pull me through,
release me from the deafening shrieks of pain.
Are you not coming, friends? You're overdue.

The walls, the beams, the nails cannot subdue
more than my flesh. In chambers of my mind
the old composers sing—they'll pull me through.
They always have. Will someone go and find

the broken fiddle bows? I want to know:
where are the children hiding? All I view
are streams of tones before blind eyes. Their flow,
I'm confident, can pull—*will* pull me through.

Ursus maritimus (Sea Bear)

You hunger for the fat-rich hide
of seal. You live to eat, to fight,
to mount, to mate. Across the wide

expanse of permafrosted white,
you trail her tracks, and can recall
that time you tasted blood and fright,

the pain of feral fangs, the brawl
with fifteen-hundred mauling pounds.
That day you were the one to fall.

And yet your prowess on these grounds
has only strengthened through the years
of earning scars and broken crowns.

You dip your head, pull back your ears,
throw wide your jaws, and hurl the roar
that all the Arctic Circle fears!

On the frozen ocean of lust and gore,
all rivals trounced, you approach the prize.
Nine feet of growling carnivore

aroused by that which liquifies
and fractures April's crystal cape,
with triumph glowing in your eyes

you rise, then boldly nip her nape
and, balanced on the glassy floe,
ease a thirst none can escape.

Two cubs are born. They'll suckle, grow
and swim and swim and swim a lot,
then face their most ferocious foe—

not bear, nor spear, nor rifle shot
but a want of ice, a home too hot.

Waiting for Dawn atop Butterfly Mountain

A dilapidated lepidopteran
dying atop The Mountain of Butterflies
holds out her wings to the darkness—wings as thin
as the mist that swirls beneath monsoonal skies—

and pictures the tea farm women, who often glow
like painted sawtooths dotting the plantation;
and, wallowing in the Mahaweli's flow,
trumpeting in carefree conversation,

elephants plashing, washing away all worry.
Unlike them, she's alone here on this rock,
a decent rock on which to dream. No hurry
to flee the fleeting memories that flock

like the birds of Sinharaja: the cunning jackal,
the whistling thrush, the fish in every lake
(which lure the hungry to come with boats and tackle
and float on magic molecules that slake

the roots of rice), the din of Devon Falls
reverberating through a green expanse
where a muntjac barks, a magpie calls and calls,
and footsteps crack the chrysalis of her trance—

men climbing toward her haven. Soon the sun
will oust the night. Slowly she beats her wings,
wings like frozen wood as, one by one,
they gain the hilltop, quicker as someone sings

a hymn to dawn, then darts away as a bell
blossoms like an orchid on the height
and, rising with the most resounding knell,
fades like the constellations at first light.

Walking with the Birds and the Bones
through Fairview Cemetery

The cardinals calling from the oaks and maples
scattered across this boneyard are my pals;
they're never flustered by the festering dead
scattered beneath the lawn. A katydid
hidden in the leaves of a sycamore
cheers me with its chirrs. The stiffs can't mar
my breezy mood provided that my ears
are titillated by these songsters' airs;
nor can the mourning dove, whose voice is sadder
than sad, coo-*ooo*-ing beyond a brake of cedar.
But as a scimitar moon and Venus gleam
and glimmer on the stones through thickening gloom,
some bird of prey unnerves the night with cries
that likely freak the phoebes, jolt the crows,
and even shock the shrikes. Above the town,
alone and hearing such an eerie tune,
I pause and think how every day I borrow
my atoms from a cosmos that will bury
my hundred trillion cells in a cemetery
whose birds insist there's nothing here that's scary
while, eyeballing me, half a dozen deer
proclaim one's thoughts should never be so dour.
From fawn to doe to buck, each barely stirs
as, one by one, the night unveils its stars.

What's for Dinner?

My parents entertain a klatch for dinner.
Ma makes everything from scratch for dinner.

She bakes potato kugel, simmers goulash,
and pan-fries blintzes (a large batch) for dinner.

A mallard leaves her eggs for just a moment.
Gulls snatch a few before they hatch (for dinner).

They're generous as all get-out, my parents,
inviting even big Sasquatch for dinner.

While love bug larvae nibble thatch for dinner,
wolves spot a moose they'll try to catch for dinner.

As Rover cleans up fallen bits of strudel,
my parents stage a shouting match for dinner.

A praying mantis gnaws her lover's noggin
somewhere in a cabbage patch for dinner.

As ma and pa begin to eat each other,
I slip out of what they unlatch for dinner.

Woodland Music

Hiking along the Lamprey River
we listened to the larks and crows,
to the leaves of birch and willow quiver,
and a thousand and one piccolos
of hot and bothered vernal peepers
merged with the warbling of brown creepers.
A distant but persistent din
began to brashly muscle in,
breaking the woodland's jocund chorus—
a mystifying hive-like hum.
We wondered where it issued from.
We thought the mountain would restore us,
reinvigorate our ears
with mountain magic, souvenirs

to take back to a megacity
whose mega noises never cease.
The youngest one among us, witty
and pert, my ever clever niece
said, "What is that unearthly droning?—
as though some animal were moaning
about how bored the trees all are.
Their sap would have more zip by far
if a gang of noxious, nauseating
ATVs zoomed down this trail."
And, sure as shooting, on our tail
they roared like a jillion chainsaws, mating
forest tune with engine noise,
a dissonance no soul enjoys—

at least not ours. We promptly scuttled
off the path as they chewed it up,
the atoms of our brains as muddled
as marbles shaken in a cup.
Inhaling fumes as they receded,
we stood there feeling quite ill-treated
but, hearing arias again
from blue jay, cardinal, and wren,
we trod anew among the cedar,
hemlock, oak, and sycamore.
Thunder! It began to pour.
Ever lighter, ever fleeter
through the sky's champagne we raced
like rabbits livened by its taste.

We made it to the old Toyota,
clothing wetter than a pond
but didn't mind it one iota,
for Earth had waved her magic wand
and doubtless had those hellions sopping—
the planet's foremost trick for stopping
such wild beasts that beat the wilds
with rumblings audible for miles.
Yet here they came again—to gall us?
Their helmets kept them nice and dry
(at least their hair). My niece, not shy,
cried out, "We came for calm and solace,
not for this ruckus you call 'fun'!"
while tires—cruel, titanic—spun

and hurtled off and left us splattered.
We drove away, smelling of muck.
I thought of all those trails, so battered,
marveled at my niece's pluck,
and wondered what the eagles, thrushes,
and others feel when a motor rushes
past a nest. Might birds desert
their eggs? Watch fledglings getting hurt?
Each thought was like the urgent squeaking
of a young, abandoned owl,
keener still with each new vowel,
till all the birds of Earth were shrieking.
And, windows shut, all nature mute,
we sped along our drizzly route.

Yellowhammer Woodpecker (Northern Flicker)

Buddy Rich never diddled a drum any quicker
than the beat of the beak of the big Northern Flicker.
Does his brain hurt? Why, no, thanks to pads in his head
as he pounds on an oak tree that's pretty well dead.

He's now rattling a tune. It rises then falls.
"We're making our nest here," he says with his calls,
then drums for his mate, each roll lasting a second.
Through his pauses, I ponder (my fancy is fecund):

If I had a look so an endearing and sweet,
snowy rump and fine black-scalloped plumage, I'd beat
out a ratamacue or a seven stroke roll
just for joy on the bark of some hollowed-out bole.

Perhaps my great drumming and looks would attract
the attention of someone to love. But, in fact,
I am happy enough merely hearing the talk
of that bird in the woods. Just to listen and walk.

Your Abstract Body

Hon, you breathe the very same air the ginkgoes
breathed as brontosauruses lumbered past them,
bending them as blusters of wind will riffle
meadows of barley.

Ancient as the galaxies, old as space-time,
hoary as the sea, but as fresh as rollers
riding bareback over the brine to borrow
some of its water,

flung from dazzling suns that have spent their rations,
cycled through the eons, your precious body
must be worth, what, hundreds of thousands, millions,
billions of dollars?

Estimate: far less than a lunch at Denny's.
You, pet, are the atoms of moons and mountains,
rushing rivers, thunderstorms, plants and planets—
common as comets.

Who, then, plays your melody? Why, the cosmos
coursing through the energy you are made of,
through the living cells of your corporation.
You are a blueprint.

Dare I fall in love with an abstract template?
Dare I not? What curious magnetism—
strong force, weak force, gravity, cosmic laughter—
draws us together!

Ballade of Mysteries

These luminous fluttering flakes of snow
are but a whit to the utterly great
sum of suns we cannot know
in the galaxies which populate
creation. Eyes that navigate
through nights as clear as infinity
itself can't begin to estimate
how huge it is. How small are we?

What spark made life so long ago,
fashioned nebulae ornate
as dahlias, galactic winds that blow
like blizzards, worlds that whirl, rotate,
makes astral A-bombs detonate,
made stars white, blue or burgundy,
caused all existence to inflate?
How huge it is! How small are we?

Snow swirls like moths in the streetlight glow,
hiding the heavens on this date,
a fiddling date in this riddling O,
an O no mind can penetrate,
where photons never gallop straight,
where clocks can't tick in synchrony,
where seeming nothingness has weight.
How huge it is! How small are we?

Space seems quite pleased to isolate
us on this rock, yet aren't we free
to feel the sun and contemplate
how huge it is? How small are we?

Notes

"A Summer Songster": "Black prince" in the envoi alludes to *Psaltoda plaga,* a species of cicada native to eastern Australia commonly known as the black prince.

"The Loneliest Road": The title alludes to Highway 50, The Loneliest Road in America. *Eagle, spider, witch-head, horsehead*, and *ghost* are names of nebulae.

"The Space Roadster": Even Elon Musk, engineer of the circus show, was surprised that his audacious stunt worked. "Apparently, there is a car in orbit around Earth," he tweeted. His plan is for the $100,000 Tesla Roadster—with the message "Don't panic!" stamped on the dashboard and David Bowie playing on the speakers—to cruise through high-energy radiation belts that circuit Earth towards deep space. —The Guardian, February 7, 2018

"Waiting for Dawn atop Butterfly Mountain": The title alludes to a mountain in south central Sri Lanka, rising to 7,359 feet (2,243 m), which is variously known as Adam's Peak (the place where Adam first set foot on earth after being cast out of heaven), Sri Pada (Sacred Footprint, left by the Buddha as he headed toward paradise), or perhaps most poetically as Samanalakande (Butterfly Mountain; where butterflies go to die). Some believe the huge "footprint" crowning the peak to be that of St. Thomas, the early apostle of India, or even of Lord Shiva.

Acknowledgments

I am grateful to the editors of the following journals and anthologies where many of these poems appeared, sometimes in earlier versions:

"An Understanding," *14 by 14;* "A Tufted Titmouse Braves a Cold Spell," "An Early Autumn Chill," "The Barking of the Dog," "Slack Traffic," "Spring Peepers," "Spring Will Leave You Behind," "The Mist," "Your Abstract Body," *Autumn Sky Poetry Daily;* "A Summer Songster," "Ballade of Mysteries," "Upheaval," "Your Abstract Body," *Better Than Starbucks;* "Cherry Blossom Reverie," "The Loneliest Road," *Cahoodaloodaling;* "Mermaids Are Waiting for You,* " *Eye to the Telescope;* "Rockledge: Winter Trails," *Inquire;* "Connecticut," *Light;* "A New Lease," "Celestial Euphony," *Lighten Up Online;* "A Preschooler Dwelleth Above," "The Mist," *Lucid Rhythms;* "A Jump-Off Place," *Mindflights;* "Somewhere Near You," *Mu Magazine;* "Snatched from the Farm: Three Sisters," *Poetry Super Highway;* "The Pigeons," *Sappho's Torque;* "Mermaids Are Waiting for You," *Scarlet Literary Magazine;* "A Link," *The Asses of Parnassus;* "The World," *The Chimaera;* "A Summer Songster," *The Flea;* "July Musings," "Pyrotechnics," "The Great Wall of America," "The Space Roadster," *The New Verse News;* "Falling More Slowly," *"*Microchiroptera," *The Oldie;* "Reservoir No. 6," "The Woolly Bear," "Walking with the Birds and the Bones through Fairview Cemetery," *The Road Not Taken;* *"*The Fledgling," *The Rotary Dial;* "Albert Einstein (1879-1955)," "Helen Keller (1880-1968)," *"*Neil

Armstrong (1930-2012)," "The Cymbal Player," "The Wright Brothers," "Waiting for Dawn atop Butterfly Mountain," *The Society of Classical Poets;* "The Fledgling," *The Speculative Edge.*

"A Summer Songster" appeared in *Some Treasures of Contemporary Rondeau Poetry;* "Cherry Blossom Reverie" appeared in *New Sun Rising: Stories for Japan;* "The Enigma of Time" appeared in *Eccentric Press Poetry Anthology, Vol. 1;* "The Loneliest Road" appeared in *Poems for a Liminal Age.*

I am grateful to the organizers of the following contests where the corresponding listed poems placed:

"Walking With the Birds and the Bones Through Fairview Cemetery" won the Thomas Gray Anniversary Poetry Competition 2014; "Microchiroptera" won The Oldie's 2013 annual bouts-rimés competition; "The Loneliest Road" was shortlisted for the Science Fiction Poetry Association's 2013 poetry contest.

Many of the poems here have either won *Poetry Nook*'s weekly poetry contests or earned an honorable mention.

I would like to thank Frank Watson, Editor-in-Chief of Plum White Press. Thanks also to the members of the Eratosphere online poetry forum.

About the Author

Martin Elster, who never misses a beat, is a percussionist with the Hartford Symphony Orchestra. Aside from playing and composing music, he finds contentment in long walks in the woods or the city and, most of all, writing poetry, often alluding to the creatures and plants he encounters.

His career in music has influenced his fondness for writing metrical verse, which has appeared in *14 by 14, Autumn Sky Poetry Daily, Better than Starbucks, Cahoodaloodaling, Eye to the Telescope, Lighten Up Online, The Centrifugal Eye, The Chimaera, The Flea, The Speculative Edge, THEMA*, and numerous other journals, e-zines, and anthologies.

His honors include *Rhymezone's* poetry contest (2016) co-winner, the *Thomas Gray Anniversary Poetry Competition* (2014) winner, the *Science Fiction Poetry Association's* poetry contest (2015) third place, and four *Pushcart* nominations.

www.ingramcontent.com/pod-product-compliance
Lightning Source LLC
Chambersburg PA
CBHW031629040426
42452CB00007B/743